ZEYDEH

ZEYDEH

tten by
oshe HaLevi Spero, Ph.D.

strated by
arilyn Hirsh

Simcha Publishing Company

Lawrence, New York

This book is dedicated to the memory of

NACHUM MAIDENBAUM z't'l

who made the words ABBA and ZEYDEH
words of beauty, warmth and understanding for us all.

Esther Maidenbaum.

Aryeh, Dassi, Rachel, Tamar, Ora, and Shalom.

Leah, Doniel, Barak, Avi, Gedaliah, Tehila, Heftzi,
Shlomo, Randi, Blanche, Rebecca, Nachum,
Hana-Leah, Benjamin, and Tiferet.

שׁירת חייו באמצע נפסקה ודם הלב
מאתנו בלא עתו הלך. איש בעל תפארת והוד
וקשה לנו הפרידה, נפלה עטת ראשנו ותפארתנו
איום המרגש וגדול הכאב, נפטר איש עדין נפש ונדיב לב
לירושלים, עיר ציון, ולשפתה הקדושה היה קשור בכל נימין

נחת לנו ולכלל ישראל מאונך והונך ביד רחבה ואדיבה
חבר נאמן לרעיתך האהובה אב מסור בעל מדות ורחמים
ובניך היו כשתילי זיתים סביב לשלחנך
מעשיך הטובים ישׂארו כסמל חי לבנך.

זכרך הטוב לא ימוש מפינו
וצמותך האצילית תעמוד לנגד עינינו לתמיד
לנצח לא נשכחך. בעלי האהוב אבינו, אחינו וסבינו

נפטר בשם טוב, בשנת ס"ה לחייו
כ"ה סיון, תשל"ט, תנצב"ה

A Note to Parents and Teachers from the Author:

Zeydeh is an honest book about death, written especially for young Jewish children. It presents, through a child's eyes, the emotional turmoil and changes in behavior which occur following the death of a loved one. It is specifically designed to provide an opportunity for the young child, ages 4 through 10 years, to experience, vicariously, the strange and sometimes confusing feelings associated with death. There are, of course, other books available for children which deal with this topic in a variety of ways; but the present book is unique in presenting this topic within the context of specific Jewish beliefs and customs dealing with death.

Zeydeh is recommended for the young child who has already raised questions about death and dying, who has experienced the loss of close relatives and friends, or who must, unfortunately, be prepared for an anticipated death in the family. It is a book which should be read to the child, or with the child, by an understanding and sensitive adult who is prepared to deal patiently with the myriad of questions, comments, and fears children have about death.

It is also important to mention that while this book provides a setting for talking about death, it intentionally does not overly philosophize about the universal question, "Why death?". This is for two reasons: First, no single explanation of death is adequate to explain all deaths. For example, the answer to why an aged person dies—he/she has lived a full life—in no way explains the death of an infant. Second, and more important, children of different ages undergo changing conceptions of the meaning, permanence, and reality of death, and thus require different levels of explanation.

Thus, while no concrete explanation of death is offered in this book - save for a very general one found on page 12 - the story should serve as a catalyst to help the child explore his/her new, almost overwhelming emotions about death together with the parent.

. . . .

In order to provide some additional guidance to parents in dealing with this topic, the following observations may be useful.

By *4 years of age, a child's notions of death are extremely limited, if he or she is concerned about it at all. At this stage, death is understood basically as an extension of life, such as sleeping or dreaming or going away for a trip. By age 5, many children begin to have a more accurate conception of death, but

---

*Please note that there is no definitive age level for any of these categories. These are only generally accepted age levels.

it is still "person-oriented" and takes the form of the angel of death or an evil man, etc. The child's basic attitude towards death expresses itself in fears of separation. By 6, children can accept the idea that death is directly associated with old age or infirmity. During the 7th year, the child becomes more fully aware of his/her own mortality. Parents begin to witness attempts, by the child, to deny his/her awareness of death. For example, sometimes children of this age will ask questions about death, and then suddenly change the topic or begin to act "silly" as soon as the parent begins to answer the questions. By the age of 8, most children become interested in a fuller explanation of what happens after death. And by 9 or 10 years, they have worked out a fairly accurate conception of death as a final, irreversible cessation of bodily processes.

In religious Jewish circles, the child's exposure to the concept of death is usually simultaneous with an introduction to our belief in **techiat ha-meisim** — the awakening of the dead during the coming of **Moshiach** (Messiah). Indeed, both concepts can be expected to undergo maturation as the child attempts to achieve a balance between the sense of the inevitability and irreversibility of death until **Moshiach** comes, and what will occur after that time.

If there are any "rules" for talking with children about death, they may be summarized as follows:

1. Always tell your child the truth - or as much of the truth as possible - rather than something fanciful that he or she will have to unlearn at a later date. At the same time, do not let the popular emphasis on demythologizing death inhibit you from talking to your child in terms of the numerous beautiful, traditional Jewish beliefs about death. For the Jew, there is a reality beyond death, and life after death; and we needn't "spare" our children such beliefs. Telling a child younger than 7 years old that a deceased loved one is "with God" is both true and comforting, as long as you are careful about giving over potentially confusing notions; i.e. "grandfather is living with God" when you have already told your child that grandfather is no longer living.

2. Never equate death with sleeping (although you might say that a dead person *looks like* he's sleeping) or taking a short trip. In younger children, such explanations will likely make them fear going to sleep or taking trips.

3. Make it very clear that a person's death is not the child's fault. In general, stay clear of the idea of "death as punishment" until children are mature enough to comprehend the meaning of this possibility.

4. Be prepared to calmly meet a child's emotional outbursts or denials of what you are saying. Repetition is preferable to forcing the issue.

5. Do not expect to tell the story of **Zeydeh** only once, or, for that matter, all at once. Children work through their anxieties and fears by repetition to any given stimulus.

6. Do not feel that you must be scientifically complete and theologically precise in your explanations. This will often overwhelm an unprepared child. In fact, children are surprisingly comfortable with parents who can honestly answer, "I don't know". On the other hand, it is often useful to respond to a child's questions by saying reflectively, "What do you think?". This will allow you to glimpse the fascinating world of your child's thinking.

7. Pay attention to signs from your child that his or her interest in the topic is waning. Reflect back to the child that it is "hard to talk a lot about some things all at once" and that "we can always talk about it again when it interests you".

8. Avoid single explanations of death (e.g., illness, sacrifice, punishment, old age), and emphasize instead that there are really several reasons for death just as there are several reasons for life.

9. When a child shows unease or exceptional preoccupation with death—demonstrated in his talk, his play, or sometimes in his conspicuous lack of interest in a death which has just occurred to a loved one—it is important to attempt to help the child express himself. A first step is to let the child know that there is nothing shameful about being afraid of death or being afraid to talk about death; and, that talking about it with someone usually makes us feel a little better. Sometimes, engaging the child in play where the parent utilizes toy animals or dolls to reenact some of the events related to the death will help a child to be more comfortable in expressing some of his feelings. Other times it may be necessary to put into words some of the fears and worries you believe the child to have, but only if you are quite sure of what the child is really thinking or feeling. If the problem persists, and the child appears to be consistently unhappy and withdrawn or otherwise different from his usual self, it may be adviseable to consult with a social worker, psychologist or rabbi experienced in this area.

10. Remember that most children have little difficulty assimilating the concept of death as long as they are patiently allowed to work with the idea and master their own worries and concerns at their own pace.

. . . .

I end this introduction on a personal note. One of the motivations in writing this book was to fill a vacuum in Jewish childrens' literature—a vacuum I felt even more keenly while attempting to explain a recent death to my own young children. The tragedy we were trying to assimilate at that time was the death of Tova Sanders Indich on Shmini Azeret 5741/1980. Together with her parents, Rabbi and Mrs. David Sanders and family, and her husband, my dear friend, Rabbi Nachum Indich, we have learned to admit the permanence of the loss of this truly beautiful young woman. But there is now an even closer and deeper wound to acknowledge. During the week that this book was being prepared for publication, my wife's family and I sacrificed a beloved son, brother, and brother-in-law. I mourn with this writing the death *al pi kiddush ha-Shem* of Daniel ben Meir Haas, a Jewish warrior with a spirit of inner peace, who perished on patrol in the Bekka Valley, Lebanon, on *Rosh Chodesh Av, 5742/1982. Tehei nishmatam zerurot be'zeror ha-hayim.*

Finally, I wish to express my gratitude to Mr. Yaacov Peterseil for undertaking to publish this innovative project, and to the Maidenbaum families for providing very generous funds for the most satisfying production and format of this book. I am also indebted to my mentor, Rabbi Mordechai Gifter, shlitah, Rosh Yeshiva of Telshe Yeshiva, who reviewed this manuscript and appreciated its value.

Moshe Halevi Spero
Cleveland Heights, Ohio
6 Shevat 5743/1983

When Zeydeh would visit us, he would sit close to me and teach me about the wonderful things in the Torah. Zeydeh would tell me many beautiful stories about great Jews who lived a long time ago.

Zeydeh would tell me about his Zeydeh.

We would take walks in my backyard and Zeydeh would tell me, in his gentle voice, what blessing to make on the different fruits and beautiful growing things that God made.

Best of all, every day when Zeydeh would pray, it was my job to bring down from the old bookcase Zeydeh's great, brown *Siddur*. Zeydeh always told me that this *Siddur* was once his Zeydeh's *Siddur*.

I felt so grown up when we prayed together from it.

I was always just a bit sad when Zeydeh would have to leave. I knew I would miss sharing things with him. But I also knew he would visit again soon.

I could hardly wait to see him.

One day I come home from school and
see Mother and Father sitting in the
living room looking very sad.

"Why are you home so early, Abba?"
I ask my father, "And why is Imah
crying?"

"I'm afraid I have sad news for you,"
Father answers. "Zeydeh died."

"Zeydeh died?" Is that what Father said? I'm not sure I know what that means. My pet hamster once died, and I cried when we buried it. But that was a hamster.

"How could Zeydeh die?" I think to myself.

Father and Mother are both crying very hard. Uncle David is calling on the phone and looks very serious. Everyone looks so sad.

I am beginning to feel sad, too.

My mother comes over and talks to me in her soft voice. "You know Zeydeh was very old, don't you?"

I nod.

"Well, when someone gets to be very old, and sometimes even when they're not really so old, they must go up to the *shamayim* and be with God."

I think for a moment and then say, "Then I want to go up to the *shamayim* with Zeydeh!"

Father tells me that what I said is what everyone feels a little bit deep inside, and it shows I love Zeydeh.

"But only God decides when you go up to the *shamayim,* " he tells me, "and God wants you to live a long time and learn to be a good person, like Zeydeh was, and do the same good deeds Zeydeh taught you."

I go up to my room and cry for a long time. I remember all the wonderful things Zeydeh and I shared together. I remember the wonderful walks . . . the nice way he talked . . . the way we prayed . . even the sweet smell of his clothes.

I still think he will come visit.

And then I cry some more.

When I come downstairs, I see lots of things around the house that belonged to Zeydeh.

When I look at his special *kiddush cup* or his special chair, I cry some more.

My mother and father say this happens to them a lot, too.

They say these special things make us think of Zeydeh. These things were part of Zeydeh so they too must be sad, now that Zeydeh is not here.

The next day we drive to the funeral where we will say goodbye to Zeydeh.

Mother says we won't be able to see Zeydeh anymore, but we can always think of him.

Father looks sad and tired. He says prayers called *Tehillim* from a *Siddur.*

he funeral is in a large hall.

ather is the first to speak.

How fortunate we are to have shared my father,
achum, with God," he says.

ather also says that after a person has done all the
ings in this world that he is supposed to do, he returns
God. This is a way of sharing with God.

It I don't feel much like sharing Zeydeh, even with God.
want to tell everyone that since God has so much already,
hy does he have to take away my grandfather too?

It I'm afraid.

ather points to a long wooden box. This is where
eydeh's body is now.

I ask Uncle David, who sits next to me, "If Zeydeh is in that wooden box how can he be with God?"

Uncle David whispers, "Zeydeh's body is in that box. His body was like a home for his soul, what we call his *neshamah*. The *neshamah* made Zeydeh's eyes sparkle and filled his mouth with Shabbat songs. And it is the *neshamah* that returns to be with God. It is only his body which we put away to rest until *Moshiach's* time."

I want to ask Uncle David about *Moshiach's* time, but first I must think about what he said some more.

After all the talks are finished, six men take Zeydeh's box outside.

The rabbi comes over and makes a small tear on the collar of Father's jacket. Father makes the tear even bigger. He makes a special blessing I never heard before: *Baruch Atah Hashem, Elokeinu Melekh ha'olam, Dayan ha'emet.*

And then he cries.

Mother sees me standing and looking at
Father. She says, "The tear *Abba* made is
like your heart breaking because you miss
Zeydeh so much. And the blessing reminds
us that no matter how sad or even angry
we feel, God is not trying to be mean or bad."

I don't know how Mother knows that I am
feeling a little bit angry at God, but it
makes me feel better to know that other
people feel this way sometimes.

I only wish I could make a tear on my
collar too.

We all go to the cemetery. I understand that this is the place where Zeydeh will be buried. It is called the *Bait Olam,* the "Forever Home". Uncle David says that Zeydeh will rest here forever.

"How long is forever?" I ask.

"Forever is until *Moshiach's* time", Uncle David answers.

"But when is that?" I ask.

Uncle David says he will tell me later.

When we come home, our neighbors, the Ramats, bring some hard boiled eggs and a piece of bread for Father to eat.

Mother tells me, "*Abba* eats an egg now because he is a mourner. A mourner is someone who has lost a close relative like Zeydeh. The mourner sees the egg is round and remembers that life is round too. First we are born, then we live our lives, then we die, and then, someday, *Moshiach* will come."

I know that this is the time to ask my question.

"Imah, what is *Moshiach's* time?"

"Moshiach's time is when those who have died will come to life again, completing the circle, like the egg."

"Will *Moshiach* come tomorrow?" I ask.

"We really don't know exactly when *Moshiach* will decide to come," she says, "but we pray he will come soon."

There is so much to think about...so much going on.. But, right now, I have another question for Mother.

"Imah, why did you cover all the mirrors in the house?"

"Well, at this sad time," she explains, "we really don't want to spend too much time looking at ourselves in th mirror, checking how our hair looks, or whether our makeup is on right. For the next seven days we really don't want to be too busy with how nice we look. We want to spend all our time thinking about Zeydeh."

"Is it okay if sometimes I think about other things?" I ask.

She smiles and says it's okay.

During the next seven days I see many more strange things happening around the house. All part of what Uncle David calls, "Sitting *Shivah*".

I see Father sitting on a low chair.

I see Father wear his torn jacket all the time.

I see Father wear slippers or no shoes at all.

"All these things," Father explains, "help me think of Zeydeh, to express my sad feelings. Do you understand?"

I say I do.

But I don't really know if I understand *"everything"*. I'll want to think about it when I'm alone.

Lots of people come to visit and talk with
Father. They don't ring the bell. They just
walk right in. Father tells me that God
wants His people to get together and
comfort each other at times like this. So,
we don't care if they don't ask permission
to come into our house now.

Everyone talks about Zeydeh and the things they remember about him.

Some of the people tell me that Zeydeh loved me very much. It makes me feel glad to hear that. I guess Zeydeh knew how much I loved him, too.

On each day of *Shivah,* many men come over in the morning, afternoon and in the night. They make sure Father has a *minyan* to pray with.

At every service Father says *Kaddish.*

"When we say *Kaddish,*" Father explains, "the *neshamah* is happy that we remembered it in our prayers. Saying *Kaddish* honors the memory of Zeydeh."

After *minyan* I collect charity, *zedakah,* from everyone.

This is a great *mitzvah.*

It reminds me of Zeydeh.

He used to collect *zedakah* too, and give it to poor people.

Just when I'm getting used to everything,
another strange thing happens.

I see Father take off his torn jacket, sit on a
regular chair, and put on his Shabbat
shoes.

"Abba, seven days aren't up yet, are they?"
I ask.

"No," he answers, "but Shabbat is coming, and during Shabbat no open signs of mourning can be shown. Of course, I still miss Zeydeh very much, but now the Shabbat Queen has arrived, and you cannot be sad when the Queen comes."

During Shabbat everything is as it used to be, except Zeydeh is not in his favorite chair anymore.

It is Shabbat, but I am still a bit sad.

At the end of the seven days, Father stops sitting on the low chair.

He puts back on his regular clothes and shoes.

This time for good.

He still looks sad and tired, but he smiles a little more now. His face looks really hairy because his beard has grown. Father explains that he will not shave or cut his hair for 30 days.

"This is another way of not being too busy with how nice we look", he says. "Another way to remember our sadness."

Once, while I am looking at a picture of Zeydeh, Father tells me, "Zeydeh loved you very much, you know."

I nod.

"But will I always remember him?" I ask.

"Yes," Father assures me, "but we are all going to have to know Zeydeh in a different way now."

"How different?" I wonder.

"Well, we'll tell stories about Zeydeh and look at pictures of him and think about all the special things he used to do and say."

"But I'll still miss him," I answer.

"We all will," says Father.

"You know, Abba, sometimes I close my eyes and think of Zeydeh. I even think I really see him. But when I open my eyes I know that Zeydeh is not here anymore. And I miss him.

Father says he has a surprise for me.

"Mother and I want you to have something that belonged to Zeydeh."

It is Zeydeh's great, brown *Siddur.*

I feel sad for a minute, like I am going to cry.

But soon I feel a special, wonderful feeling.

ZEYDEH'S SPECIAL *SIDDUR!*

Zeydeh and I shared this *Siddur* when we prayed together.

And Zeydeh once told me this *Siddur* belonged to his Zeydeh.

And now it's mine.

When I become a Zeydeh, I will share this *Siddur* with my grandchildren.

Glossary:

Abba . . . . Father

Bait Olam . . . . Cemetery; literally, eternal home

Imah . . . . Mother

Kaddish . . . . Doxology, or the prayer said by mourners
in praise of God

Kiddush . . . . The sanctification over wine. A "Kiddush Cup"
is the cup used for Sabbath and holiday
sanctification ritual

Minyan . . . . A group of 10 males necessary for group prayer
and recitation of Kaddish

Mitzvah . . . . A religious duty

Moshiach . . . . Messiah

Neshamah . . . . The soul or spirit

Shamayim . . . . The heavens

Shivah . . . . The first seven days of mourning
following burial

Siddur . . . . Prayer book

Tehillim . . . . Psalms

Zedakah . . . . Charity

Zeydeh . . . . Grandfather (Yiddish)

Selected Bibliography of Books dealing with Death for children and Adults:

Abbott, Sarah: **The Old Dog.** New York: Coward, McCann & Geoghegan, 1972.

Anthony, Sylvia: **The Discovery of Death.** New York: Basic Books, 1972.

Bartoli, Jennifer: **Nonna.** New York: Harvey House, 1975.

Bernstein, Joanne & Gullo, Stephen V.: **When People Die.** New York: E.F. Dutton, 1977. (Explicit photographs with supportive text.)

Brown, Margaret Wise: **The Dead Bird.** Mass.: Young Scott, 1958.

Burton, L. (ed): **Care of the Child Facing Death.** London: Routledge & Kegan Paül, 1974. (Excellent guide for parents and teachers.)

Carrick, Carol: **The Accident.** New York: Seabury Press, 1976. (A boy's beloved dog is accidentally killed and he learns to deal with his rage and sadness.)

Carlson, Natalie: **The Half Sisters.** New York: Harper & Row, 1970. (For 8-12 year olds; a girl learns to accept the death of her sister.)

de Paola, Tommie: **Nana Upstairs, Nana Downstairs.** New York: P. Putnam's Sons. (For 5-10 year olds; a boy deals with the death of two grandparents.)

Dobrin, A.: **Scat.** New York: Four Winds Press, 1971.

Donovan, John: **I'll Get There: It Better Be Worth the Trip.** New York: Harper & Row, 1971. (11-14 year olds.)

Easson, W.M.: **The Dying Child.** Springfield, Ill.: Charles C. Thomas, 1970.

Fassler, Joan: **My Grandpa Died Today.** New York: Human Sciences Press, 1971.

Fenton, Edward: **A Matter of Miracles.** New York: Holt, 1967. (11-14 years old.)

Forrai, Maria: **A Look At Death.** Minn.: Lerner Publications, 1978. (Realistic photographs.)

Furman, Erna: **A Child's Parent Dies.** New Haven: Yale University Press, 1974. (An extremely erudite, clinical analysis of the issue of children's ability and ways of dealing with and accepting death.)

Gordon, Audrey & Klass, Dennis: **They Need to Know: How to Teach Children About Death.** New Jersey: Prentice-Hall, 1979. (For parents and educators.)

Green, Phyllis: **A New Mother for Martha.** New York: Human Sciences Press, 1978.

Grollman, Earl A.: **Explaining Death to Children.** Boston: Beacon, 1967. (A classic text with insightful essays and bibliographies for parents.)

Grollman, Earl A.: **Talking About Death: A Dialogue Between Parent and Child.** Boston: Beacon, 1976. (Poetic text with abstract illustrations that invite the child's fantasies.)

Harris, Audrey: **Why Did He Die?** Minn.: Lerner House, 1965

Hoopes, Lyn L.: **Nana.** New York: Harper & Row, 1981. (Poetic and sensitive.)

Jackson, Edgar: **Telling a Child About Death.** New York: Hawthorne, 1965. (Another classic and skillful guide for parents.)

Kantrowitz, Mildred: **When Violet Died.** New York: Parents Magazine Press, 1973.

Kremmentz, Jill: **How It Feels When A Parent Dies.** New York: Knopf, 1981. (An interesting approach which utilizes self-report dialogue from children of ages 7-16 years old.)

Lee, V.: **The Magic Moth.** New York: Seabury Press, 1972.

LeShan, Eda: **Learning to Say Goodbye.** New York: McMillan, 1976. (For older children and parents.)

Michell, M.E.: **The Child's Attitude Toward Death.** New York: Schocken, 1967.

Miles, Miska: **Annie and the Old One.** Boston: Little, Brown, 1971.

Mohr, Nicholosa: **Nilda.** New York: Harper & Row, 1973. (11-14 years old.)

Riemer, Jack: **Jewish Reflections on Death.** New York: Schocken, 1974. (Insightful. Of mostly philosophical nature.)

Rosenthal, Ted.: **How Could I Not Be Angry At You?** New York: Braziller, 1973. (11-14 years old.)

Schector, Ben: **Across the Meadow.** New York: Doubleday, 1973

Simmons, Bernadette: **But She's Still My Grandmother!** New York: Human Sciences Press, 1982.

Smith, Doris B.: **A Taste of Blackberries.** New York: Crowell, 1973.

Stein, Sara B.: **About Dying.** New York: Walker & Co., 1974. (Photographs to be shared by family; a child discovers the meaning of death by dealing with the death of a bird and then her grandmother.)

Tresselt, Alvin: **The Dead Tree.** New York: Parents Magazine Press, 1972. (8-12 years old.)

Viorst, Judith: **The Tenth Good Thing About Barney.** New York: Atheneum, 1971. (A child comes to terms with the death of his cat.)

Warburg, Sandol: **Growing Time.** Boston: Houghton-Mifflin, 1969.

Zeligs, Rose: **Children's Experiences With Death.** Springfield, Ill: Charles C. Thomas, 1975. (For parents and educators.)

Zolotow, Charolette: **My Grandson Lew.** New York: Harper & Row, 1974.